Introduction

For quite a few years now, I have been interested in history, local history especially from the first time I discovered that Sheffield had two castles, I was fascinated. I wanted to learn more which I did in various ways; obviously I am still learning new things about Sheffield's history, and I suppose I always will be.

What I have aimed to do in this particular 'presentation' is briefly to inform not only the tourist or visitor about Sheffield's history, but also the local, the 'Sheffielder'.

Some people will already know a bit or maybe even a lot about the times that I have chosen to write about. For all those who are not familiar with these particular times I hope that you will be as fascinated / interested as when I learned for the very first time of these events. Today I am still both fascinated and interested.

I have also included photographs of some of the events that I have written about.

David Saville

Centuries ago, around where Castle Market stands today, a forest was partly cleared. It was cleared to enable the Saxons to create a site on which to erect their dwellings, commonly using 'wattle and daub'. The site was known as a clearing, or a 'feld'; the feld was situated at the side of the River Sheaf, (Saxon pronunciation 'Sceath'),(any word using the letters 'SC' in it were pronounced 'SH'), therefore the two words pronounced together, the 'SCEATH', by the 'FELD' – (Sheffield).

Any place names such as Stannington, Beighton, or Owlerton would have in Saxon times been Enclosed Farmsteads, as the word 'TON' meant 'Enclosed Farmstead', any place name with 'LEY' on the end of it, such as Tinsley, or Totley etc, would have been in Saxon times – Clearings in the Forest, as the word meant 'Clearings in the Forest'.

In the 11th century, Saxon Earl Walthoef was in control of the lands around 'Hallun' or Hallam as we know it to date, in his time Waltheof, along with other Saxon Earls in England, planned rebellions against William the Conqueror. At first William forgave Waltheof, and even allowed him to marry his niece, Countess Judith. Waltheof later went too far so to speak, by plotting another Rebellion. William heard of this new plot whilst putting down a Rebellion back in Normandy. He was furious; William on his return to England (England meant 'Land of the Anglo Saxon'), found Waltheof guilty, as the other Saxon Earls had blamed the whole plot on Waltheof.

Waltheof this time wasn't so fortunate; William had Waltheof beheaded outside the walls of the City of Winchester on the 30th May 1076, the only Englishman to be beheaded by William. Waltheof was buried at Crowland Abbey in the remote Lincolnshire Fens.

With Waltheof dead, his lands passed to Countess Judith; his name is remembered today by Waltheof School, just off the Sheffield Parkway.

Around this time Roger De Busli, a Norman Knight from Huntingdon, had earlier sailed across the Channel with William the Conqueror and was rewarded for his services by receiving numerous 'Estates', now Roger De Busli was made principal tenant of the land which Countess Judith had inherited on the death of her husband, Waltheof.

Roger however lost interest in the lands of which Countess Judith had made him principal tenant; he left Escafeld (Sheffield) for Tickhill where he built his 'Motte' and 'Bailey' castle. Roger had been Sheffield's first Norman Lord.

Later the Medieval family of Lovetot arrived. There were three generations of the Lovetots which spanned around one hundred years. It is strongly thought that the

Lovetots made the early making of Sheffield as a Town.

Around 1100 William De Lovetot erected a Motte and Bailey Castle, now Castle Markets. His castle was built on what is thought to have been Saxon Earl Waltheof (Aula) Hall. This was a timber framed structure and its remains still exist beneath the market today. Some historians have agreed that his (Aula) Hall was in Hallun (Hallam today).

The Lovetots would have dug a ditch around their castle, the earth from the ditch creating the mound that the Castle was to sit on. A fence is thought to have been added around the stronghold around 1150, a Church and a Corn mill were also erected around the area of Millsands, near Lady's Bridge.

A hospital is believed to have stood in the area of Spital Hill, but to my knowledge no evidence of that building has ever been discovered. The ancient name for this Hospital was Spital, this is how Spital Hill and Spital Fields got their names. Just below Spital Hill we have the Wicker part of Sheffield, a flat piece of land, which centuries ago was known as Sembly Green; here Town meetings were held as well as where criminals were tried etc. Archery practice also took place here; the archery targets known as wickers, are thought to have given this part of Sheffield its name - the other reason is thought to have originated from women making wicker baskets, using reeds from the side of the river. Imagine then, if you stood in the Wicker / Lady's Bridge or Market areas today and picture the Warriors / Bowmen walking from the Castle over the bridge down to Sembly Green (Wicker), with their Bows and Arrows for an Archery tournament.

A Chapel on the Wicker side of the bridge (Lady's), stood at the foot of the bridge centuries ago (St. Leonard's); because of the Chapel the Bridge was named The Bridge of our Lady Virgin Mary, later to be shortened to the name we know it as today, Lady's Bridge. Beneath today's modern Lady's Bridge is a stone arched bridge dating from 1486.

In the foundations of the old Sheaf Market (now demolished) there is a stone-arched bridge which dates from 1596; this replaced an earlier bridge made from wood which was situated over the River Sheaf. Today this part of the River Sheaf is covered over with the foundations of the old Sheaf market for a start.

The lands later passed to the Furnivals, with the marriage of Maud De Lovetot to Gerard De Furnival. A road in Attercliffe remembers this Medieval Family (Lovetot Road).

Gerard De Furnival was killed in the crusades in Palestine around 1213 – 1215. Then followed *five* Lord Thomas De Furnivals; the first Thomas was also killed in the crusades - he was brought back to England. Thomas was buried in Worksop Priory; he was followed later by his mother Maud, and his three sisters.

2nd Lord Thomas De Furnival:
It was during this Lord's time that the Simon De Montfort rebellion took place; it was a Baron's rebellion against the Bad Rule of Henry III. A supporter of Simon De Montfort's rebellion was a man named John De Eyvill; his forces on the way to Derbyshire sacked and burned the little Town of Sheffield along with the Lovetot's Motte and Bailey Castle in 1266.
Sheffield at that time comprised the Castle (Castle Market) with one road (High Street) up to where Sheffield Cathedral stands today.

Because of the attack on Sheffield, the culprits were slaughtered at Chesterfield.

Now the 2nd Lord Thomas De Furnival was granted permission to rebuild a Castle of stone in 1270 to replace the one destroyed in 1266 (4 years prior). Henry III granted this rebuilding of the Castle to Thomas because Thomas supported the King during the Baron's rebellion which led to the burning of Sheffield.

A stone Castle was erected over the destroyed Castle, (the Saxon hall reputedly beneath that), the site was situated at the Confluence of the River's Dun and Sheaf (Dun being the old name for Don).

The Lady's Bridge side of the Castle had a natural defence by the way of the river and its low lying river cliffs. There was the hill leading from the river up to the Castle; this part is now covered by Castlegate, around the rest of the Castle - Waingate (now landscaped and built up), a ditch / moat was dug; this continued right around the Castle, where the site of Mace's Pet Shop was once situated and carried on past where the Market Tavern pub stands today, then it rejoined the river once more where the Spiral Walkway leads into the back end of Castle Market.

Imagining that Castle Market is the site of our ancient Castle, lets add the ditch / moat to go all the way round it apart from the Lady's Bridge side - don't forget this was a natural defence; when I write about this moat, I don't mean a narrow shallow affair, but a GREAT DITCH, one which is said to have been around 30ft wide and 18ft deep, probably Stone lined to help keep the water in. This is thought to have part of it built on; the building I refer to is the original Town Hall, and later the Crown Court building on the Waingate Side - both are the same building.

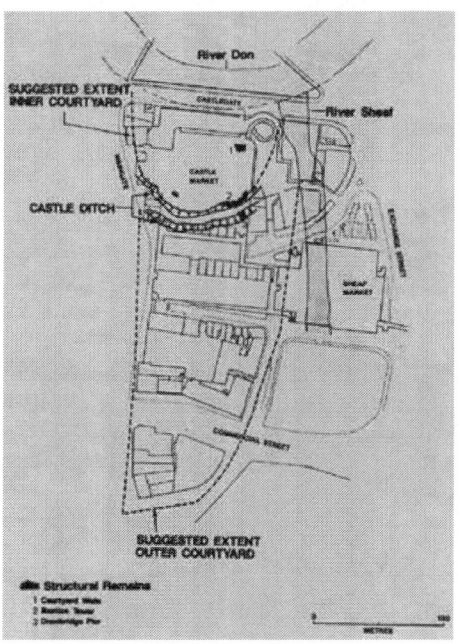

Back to the castle itself, some of its walls are said to have been around 4 yards thick, its drawbridge around where the Market Tavern pub stands today. Foundations of the 'Drawbridge Pier' are said to survive below ground; it's thought that the Castle ran right the way up to where the Primark store is today (once the C & A store); it was possibly one of the Major Strongholds in the North of England.

The Castle Barns are thought to have stood where the Wilkinson store stands today.

Sometime after the Barns came the Tontine Inn Stagecoach company. Tontine Inn was bought by the Duke of Norfolk in 1850; he then had the building demolished, then erected the Norfolk Market hall (also now demolished).

In 1296, Lord Thomas De Furnival (3rd Furnival) was granted a market charter by Edward I; this meant that a market could be held every week on a Tuesday and a fair during three days of the 'Holy Trinity'.

Lord Thomas De Furnival (4th Furnival) was Lord of Hallam for around 7 years; he died at Sheffield Castle, he was laid to rest at Beauchief Abbey in Sheffield.

Lord Thomas De Furnival (5th Furnival) died childless and was therefore followed by his brother William.

William and his wife Thomasine had one child, this child was a daughter by the name of Joan. In later years Joan married Sir Thomas De Neville; they too had a daughter, by the name of Maud. She eventually married John Talbot (Earl of Shrewsbury), the Furnival's estate passing to the Earls of Shrewsbury. The Furnival family are remembered today by places such as Furnival Road, Furnival Gate, Furnival Way and Furnival House.

The 4th Earl of Shrewsbury (George Talbot) erected part of the Manor Lodge / Castle in Sheffield on the site of a Medieval Hunting lodge in about 1520; today the tomb of the 4th Earl can be viewed in the Shrewsbury Chapel, Sheffield Cathedral (formerly St. Peters and St. Paul's). Either side of him his two wives lie, Ann and Elizabeth. The Tomb is 'Alabaster'; the 4th Earl died at Wingfield Manor in 1538.

Francis (5th Earl of Shrewsbury) was born at Sheffield Castle in the year 1500, Sheffield's Manor Lodge was erected by the 4th Earl of Shrewsbury (George Talbot), because it is said that Sheffield Castle was too overcrowded due to the large family of Talbots.

The most outstanding Earl of Shrewsbury must be George Talbot the 6th Earl, the Lord of Manor Lodge Sheffield; he had one or two other residences including Sheffield Castle and was made custodian to Mary Queen of Scots by order of Elizabeth I. George first brought Mary to Sheffield on November 28th 1570 - she was a Royal prisoner in Sheffield for just under 14 years. This was the longest time she'd stopped in any one place whilst being held in captivity; she left Sheffield on the 2nd September 1584. During these 14 years she was held at Sheffield Castle where it is said she would ride around the Castle grounds on a horse and cart. She had odd breaks at the Manor Lodge, Buxton, Chatsworth and Worksop.

Sheffield Castle was set in 8 acres of land near to a substantial amount of Moorland; it must have been quite a breathtaking scene of the day at the very least.
At the Manor Lodge it is said that Mary would take to the Turret House roof for fresh air and to watch the deer grazing.

Whilst at the Castle of Sheffield, Mary & George wrote of an Earthquake - only a minor one, but enough for what this country was used to; it shook the buildings. This earthquake was said to have happened on the 26th

February 1575. Mary also wrote that her women could not work around her, because they could not sit steady or properly on their chairs; maybe Mary was referring to the women that were sewing, which was common practice at this time.

George Talbot the 6th Earl of Shrewsbury was married to Bess of Hardwick; he was her 4th husband and her his 2nd wife. Great strain was put on the marriage because of George Talbot being the Queen of Scots' custodian. George and Bess later separated; Bess had outlived 3 husbands, and was to eventually outlive George. Bess's residences were Hardwick Hall, and Haddon Hall; there were 2 Hardwick Hall's (the 2nd was built for Bess of Hardwick) though it is said she didn't get to live there until obviously the building work was completed. She was 77 when she finally moved in. She was the richest woman in England after Elizabeth I.

George Talbot died at the Manor Lodge in November 1590. His tomb is opposite the tomb of the fourth Earl of Shrewsbury in the Shrewsbury Chapel (Sheffield Cathedral), formerly St. Peter's and St. Paul's.

George Talbot it is said is not actually in the tomb, but beneath it. The funeral of this 6th Earl was said to have drawn quite a crowd; so large was the crowd all trying to get a glimpse of the coffin, that people climbed trees nearby to see. Unfortunately branches of a tree gave way killing a few people and injuring many more.

Gilbert 7th Earl of Shrewsbury was a very bad tempered individual to say the least. There were many folk of Sheffield who were poor; at the same time Gilbert lived a very charmed well-to-do lifestyle.

After the death of Gilbert in 1616, it was found in his will that a hospital was to be built for so many of Sheffield's poor towns folk. But there was a problem; it was found that there was no money for the said building. This project was put on hold if you will, right upto 1665 when Gilbert's grandson supplied the money needed for the hospital, and it was named Talbot Earl of Shrewsbury Hospital. It took until 1825 - it was situated on the site of today's Park Square roundabout near Castle Market, Sheffield City Centre.

The Talbots Earls of Shrewsbury are remembered today by amongst other things both Talbot Road and Shrewsbury Road / Street.

Mary Queen of Scots is remembered by amongst other things Queen Mary Road on the Manor in Sheffield, the Captive Queen public house, Sheffield and Queen Mary's room (a room situated in the Turret House Manor Lodge, Manor Lane, Manor Sheffield).

In 1642 the English Civil War broke out and in 1644

Sheffield Castle came under siege. The attackers were the Parliamentarians, the defenders in the Castle being the Royalists. Sheffield's townsfolk helped the Parliamentarian's soldiers in a few ways including erecting a camp close to Sheffield Park, and assisting with the building of a defensive wall of sods and stones. A tricky business it must have been then because the Royalists (the Defenders) were firing on the builders of the sods and stones defensive wall whilst the wall was being erected.

The practice of tunnelling under a Castle Moat and / or under the castles entrance had been a common practice centuries before the English Civil War.

The Parliamentarians tried tunnelling under the moat of Sheffield castle; they were unsuccessful and the idea was soon brought to a halt, the reason being they hit upon solid rock and obviously no way through it.

A shot from a cannon severely damaged a wall on one side of 2nd Lord Thomas De Furnival's Castle of 1270. It is said that stone from the walls came hurtling down into the water of the moat.
Eventually by the 10th / 11th August 1644, there were no Royalist soldiers left in the Castle apart from a group who had come across quite a quantity of ale. These were quickly taken prisoner after a swift raid on the castle. The majority of the Royalist soldiers had eventually

Remains of 'Old' 'Sheffield Castle'
Castle Markets, Sheffield
(Gatehouse Tower?)
1999
Photo by David Saville

A 'Test Trench' by Sheffield
University student Archaeologists
'The Dig' was in part of 'Old' 'Sheffield Castles' 'Moat'
Nearing the bottom of the 'Moat'
20ft below surface of bottom loading bay
Castle Markets 1999
Photo by David Saville

Top: From left to right
1. Saxon Earl Waltheof
2. William De Lovetot
3. Gerard De Furnival

Bottom: From left to right
4. Thomas De Nevil
5. John Talbot
6. John Bright

Sheffield Cathedral

Photo by David Saville

An Archaeologist in 'The Test Trench'
This is/was dug in part of 'Old' Sheffield Castles' 'Moat'
This is was dug by student Archaeologists
from Sheffield University
Castle Markets 1999
Photo by David Saville

Ruins of Gatehouse Tower?
Castle Market
Sheffield City Centre, 1999
Photo by David Saville

River 'Sheaf'
Near back end of Pond Street, 2000
Photo by David Saville

Ruins of Gatehouse Tower?
Which was once part of Sheffield 'Stone' Castle,
Castle Market, Sheffield City Centre, 1999
Photo by David Saville

The Old Manor Castle/ Lodge 'Middings'
Once used by Mary Queen of Scots?
25th September, 1999
Photo by David Saville

An Archaeological dig
on 'Sheffield Castle' moat
Sheffield 'Castle Markets', 1999
Photo by David Saville

Re- enactors in front of
The Turret House, Manor 'Castle' Sheffield
25th September, 1999 (Saturday)
Photo by David Saville

Archaeologists/ Students from Sheffield University
in the middle of a 'Test Trench'
The 'Dig' is in part of 'Old' 'Sheffield Castle' 'Moat'
Castle Markets, Bottom loading bay
1999 Sheffield City Centre
Photo by David Saville

'George Talbot' '6th Earl Shrewsburys' Tomb'
in Shrewsbury Chapel (Sheffield Cathedral)
Photo by David Saville

Ruins of 'Old' Sheffield Castle
Top right of photo and the stone below
it have markings. These may be due to the sharpening
of 'Arrowheads' etc, Castle Markets, 1999
Photo by David Saville

The start of a 'Test Dig'
on part of 'Old' Sheffield Castle
'Moat' by Sheffield University students. Bottom loading bay
Sheffield Castle Markets, 1999
Photo by David Saville

Remains of Gatehouse Tower, Castle Market
These ruins are located at the end
of the meat and fish market. 2000
Photo by David Saville

Ruins of Manor Lodge/ Castle. 1998
Photo by David Saville

A 'Test Dig' on part of 'Old' Sheffield Castle
'Moat' by Sheffield University students
Bottom loading bay
Sheffield Castle Markets, 1999
Photo by David Saville

Remains of 'Old' Sheffield ('Stone')Castle 12- 70 1648
Glass case on floor holding a charred piece of timber
which is said to be from the first castle (earth and wood built)
Around 1100 - 1266. Earth and wood castle
was originally on the same spot as where stone
castle was later built. Earth and wood castle attacked and
burned down 1266
1999, Photo by David Saville

'Waltheof' School
Named after 'Saxon Earl 'Waltheof'
Just off 'Sheffield Parkway'
1999?
Photo by David Saville

Remains of 'Old'
'Sheffield Castle'
Castle Markets, Sheffield
White walls are modern
1999
Photo by David Saville

These are some of the 'Remains' of Sheffield Stone Castle
(Gatehouse Tower?)
This castle was built in 1270 by Thomas De Furnival
Demolished after English civil war in 1648
12th December 2000
Photo by David Saville

Remains of 'Old' 'Sheffield Castle'
Castle Markets, Sheffield
(Gatehouse Tower?)
1999
Photo by David Saville

Looking down onto Castle Gate from loading bay car park
(Castle Market)
on left:- A Pub,
middle:- Magistrates Court
on right:- Old Lady's Bridge (modern)
below modern (Old Bridge, oldest bridging
point in Sheffield, Built (1486) in stone
1999
Photo by David Saville

surrendered earlier and were allowed to leave the castle with their flags flying marching and playing their drums; these ordinary soldiers were allowed to go home providing they laid down their arms, swords, pistols etc. Officers could go where they wanted and were allowed to keep their horse, sword and pistol.

Sheffield Castle became a Parliamentarian stronghold, Colonel John Bright was made governor of the castle; soon though John was to be made governor of Hull and York. A Captain Edward Gill that came from Norton was to take over the command at Sheffield Castle.

Colonel John Bright had lived at Carbrook Hall (now a public house and said to be the most haunted in Sheffield, John Bright being the ghost). He also held many a Parliamentarian meeting at Carbrook Hall. A building is said to have stood on the site of Carbrook Hall centuries before when a family by the name of Blunt, occupied the site back in 1176.

The Earl of Arundel was allowed to buy the castle for £6000; the castle must have been in a very ruinous state to say the least, along with the estate. On saying that the Earl of Arundel could buy back the castle, Parliament had other ideas.

In 1646 a resolution was passed, this resolution being for Sheffield Castle to be sleighted and demolished. The reason being so that the castle could never pose a threat as a stronghold as it had already done by the Royalists, and so in 1648 the castle was sadly demolished with the stone etc. being sold off to local townsfolk.

Years later a poet by the name of Francis Buchanan wrote a poem about how he and the Sheffield's townsfolk felt about losing Sheffield Castle. He paid great tribute to the castle and about how great it must have been with its great towers etc. He asks the castle in his poem where its great towers are, where are thy great battlements, buttresses and hall; the poem was written sometime in the 1800s. I think it sums up the tragic end to what must have been a great piece of Sheffield history. Read it yourself and see what you think. The castle of stone had stood 378 years.

The castle site was later covered over and the moat filled in, the site having since been used for a wide range of things including our present Castle Market from the 20th century (1900s)

The castle was so thoroughly demolished that all that remains of this once great castle is what is said to be the ruin of the gatehouse tower; this is situated in a room at the top loading bay of Castle Market.

As you walk up the spiral walkway on Exchange Street at the rear of the market, you will see a door on your right just before you go through the rear door entrance to the market; above this door are the words 'Sheffield Castle Ruins'. These can be viewed by an appointment usually to be made at the customer information centre or the 5th floor of the Market's office block.

Other castle remains lie beneath the Market - these are no longer open to the public because it is said that there is a build up of poisonous gas from time to time and obviously dangerous. Other ruins I will inform you of later.

During the castles demolition a large flag stone was found with the words ' I Lord Furnival, I Built this hall and beneath this wall was my burial'.

A stone coffin was also found. It is said that the body remains were tipped out and the coffin taken up to the Manor Lodge and used as a horse trough. Today a stone coffin stands outside the Turret House up at the Manor Lodge Sheffield.

In Fitzalan Square Sheffield City Centre is the old post office building; it is said that vast slopes ran down to the river sheaf around today's Pond's Forge etc. In around 1910 it is reputed that the slopes were built up in order to run tram cars up and down. If you stand outside the former post office today you will notice that around the area of the old Halfords shop near the taxi rank (top of Pond Hill) the ground still goes on a gentle slope. This slope carries on right the way past where you would be stood, then carries on to where the old steps are; the slope carries on after the steps and down to the area of Pond's Forge.

Down to the Pond Street of today, at the side of the ever-changing bus station stands the old Queen's Head public house. It is not the oldest public house in Sheffield as thought by quite a few people; it is however reputed to be the oldest timber-framed building in Sheffield. It is thought the building was once the wash house for Sheffield Castle; it is also thought that the building was part of the castle's estate.

Centuries ago the building was known as the 'Hawle by the Pondes' (hall by the ponds); the hall was named so because of the ponds that are thought to have been situated by it.

It is also reputed that there were mills on the site of today's Pond Street. Some of these mills are thought to have been making arrow heads at the time and for the battle of Agincourt in the 1400's.

Gun Lane in the Wicker so it is said got its name because of a cannon which was stood on this area aimed at the walls of the castle during the English Civil War. Remember there were no buildings stood on the Wicker near Lady's Bridge, or on the bridge itself, not like buildings we know of or like we have today.

The area around Haymarket situated between Castle Market and Fitzalan Square centuries ago was known as Bullstake, this is where the town bull is said to have been hired out from.

The market cross is said to have been placed somewhere in what is High Street today, Sheffield City Centre. This cross marked where the market square stood centuries ago, right outside the castle walls; this is so because beyond the castle and moat (the site of our castle market), the castle carried on right up to where Primark is today (old C & A store); just across the way from Primark we have Castle Square.

Irish cross is thought to have been at the bottom of where Snig Hill is today, said to be where foreigners could sell their wares. Today Castle House Store and Argos Superstore etc stand here, just around the corner from Castle Market.

Years ago workmen carrying out a job in connection with the main drainage system of Sheffield had to carry work out through Castle Hill. A tunnel was located at quite a depth below the level of the ground at the time; it is said that the tunnel was 18ft below Waingate. At the time of the discovery of the tunnel there was a company by the name of Messrs C. Chambers & Co. and it was thought that the tunnel could have been 40ft below their backyard, under the River Sheaf, just above the weir. This was at the back of the Alexandra Music Hall along or across Castle Hill; it went along to the end of Bridge Street.

When they had tunnelled under the river bit by bit, they went through a loose section deposited by water, the workmen it is said found quite a few bones and other remains; some of these were deer antlers.

When they got to the Castle Hill stage of the job they came upon rock, looking like what is called Handsworth Stone; it is said that it was very finely grained and of a bluish colour.

The blasting through of the rock was to make the sewer - two shafts were then sunk, one in Messrs C. Chambers & Co.'s yard, and the other near Waingate. The workmen having done the sinking on Castle Hill cut across another passage which had already been there to start with, excavated out of the tough solid rock.

On running towards the market hall it was quite hard to judge whether it carried on to the Manor. The passage was quite blocked with rubble but even so it was still around 4 or 5 ft in height with its roof totally unmarred. Unfortunately the mystery of where it led to was never investigated; as usual, time was against the workmen. The passage stuck in people's minds from then on because investigations were proposed from time to time but it is said that no investigation was ever done.

When the shaft was filled a wall of debris and rubble was built right the way across the tunnel to stop the loose material falling into it, and the men then left it in what must have been a dark and damp atmosphere.

The second shaft was sunk to about 25ft; there a wall was discovered, but because the wall was in the way of where the men needed to work, part of it was sadly taken away.

In all 3 or maybe 4 walls were discovered, the 1st is what was thought to have been around 10ft thick and at a guess could very well have been an outer wall rather that an inner wall.

The 2nd again at a guess is said to have been around 6ft thick, the 3rd around 3 ¼ ft thick.

The plinth stones at the original level of the ground seemed to have been 20ft below the level of the 1800s. This surface was to slope downhill towards the river.

In 1999 archaeologists carried out an investigation to try and discover the kinds of things being thrown out of the castle etc. by its different occupants centuries ago. As well as a defensive feature the moat / ditch was used like a big rubbish bin, so the dig was on the bottom loading bay of Castle Market.

It was on part of the old moat, as they removed the lid off part of the moat they soon came upon what looked like to me as being old floors of Victorian back yards as there were rocks and stones laid neatly in 2 or 3 rows.

Personally I don't think they had anything to do with the old castle as they seemed too near to the present day's surface.

Further and further down the archaeologists went with their buckets trowels etc. After a few weeks of careful investigations and excavations they reached the very bottom of that section of moat, it was around 20ft deep, in the 6 weeks (or thereabouts) of the dig, rocks and stones which were more likely to have been from the old castle judging by the depth they were discovered.

Pieces of glazed floor tile a brownish colour with a yellowy decorative pattern were found, thought to have been part of the Great Hall which stood in the mighty Sheffield Castle once upon a time.

Clothes pins were found along with other finds. The site of the dig was eventually filled in again.

Around 2001 – 2002 another dig was carried out by archaeologists this time on the top loading bay of Castle

Market, just around the corner from the earlier dig, on your right as you go through the back entrance of Castle Market, on the spot that houses part of the castle ruins.

What looked like a small section of courtyard was found (cobbled), the cobbles were laid in the ground, a base of what looked like a tower was also discovered, and it was shaped very much like a 50p piece. Stone steps of some kind were also discovered.

Over the other side of the top loading bay another dig was underway; although this dig was on a much larger scale, both the digs were just as exciting as each other. This larger dig was set back a little way from the long concrete wall between the 2 pubs the Alexandra and the other one near Lady's Bridge which has amongst other names been called Tap and Spile.

In this particular excavation the archaeologists came across a section of walls, which could have been part of the Curtain Wall, (the outer wall of the Castle), as a hill or embankment sloped away from the wall to the river in this area centuries ago; this was long before the road we know as Castlegate today.

The smaller excavation near the back entrance to Castle Market was filled with sand, one reason for this being so that future digs could be carried out more quickly and easily. At the moment these ruins lay filled in again, sandwiched between the ground of the top loading bay and behind the long concrete wall situated on Castlegate, Sheffield. This dig was visited by the Sheffield Star Newspaper, Calendar News, Lord Mayor Baker and Lady Mayoress Baker.

The dig lasted a few weeks, around the area of Smithfield car park, where car boot sales are held on a Sunday just across from Castle Market. This area was said to be occupied by orchards, a hopyard, and a cockpit, centuries ago.

Findings from the historic site on which Castle Market stands today include belt buckles, bone dice, a piece of window tracery, stirrups, a sword and a pair of typical Medieval pointed shoes (in black). These were found in the silt of the River Don so the old story goes and are thought to be over 700 years old!!!! These are on show in a glass cabinet in Weston Park Museum.

Apart from these findings the site has never really been excavated.

 Between 1927 to 1930 a man named Armstrong made a quick survey of the site, rumour has it his wife was very ill and he could no longer carry through the work.

In 1996 on the Gallery at Castle Market an Exhibition Centre was set up, this was to mark 700 years of Sheffield's markets , it was also to celebrate the anniversary of (3rd) Thomas De Furnival's market charter being granted to him by Edward I back in 1296.

In this centre around the edge of the room there were information boards about Sheffield through the centuries, including the Saxons, two Castles, the Talbot's (Earls of Shrewsbury), Mary Queen of Scots, the English Civil War and various markets such as Norfolk Market Hall, Corn Exchange, Castle Market, Sheaf Market, Rag & Tag market, Parkway Market, Crystal Peaks, plus The Moor.

A television screen showed ruins of the stone castle, the ones no longer visited by the public because of the poisonous gas and also those in the room near the back entrance to Castle Market. Two bells stood on the floor of the exhibition centre, one from the old Corn Exchange, the other being from The Norfolk Market Hall. A visit to the ruins in the room on the top loading bay was also included; merchandise or souvenirs were also on sale, for example, pens, pencils, rulers, key rings, T-Shirts, caps, erasers and pin badges. Alas the exhibition centre closed, though all the information boards etc remained. The Centre was opened on request or by appointment only and this included the castle ruins.

The Centre was finally dismantled; where the information boards finally ended up I am not quite sure, I was very disappointed to see the centre go. The castle ruins can still be visited by making an appointment at the customer information centre or the office on the 5th floor; both are within the establishment of Castle Market.

At the back of the Sadacca building in the Wicker there is an information board, this tells a little of Sheffield's history regarding the Castles, The Wicker, also the nature and wildlife in this area.

On Lady's Bridge, there is an information board - this is a brief historical piece regarding the Bridge, Medieval times, Mary Queen of Scots etc; on the end of the concrete wall on Castlegate there is a small silver plaque near the spiral walkway, informing people briefly about a Saxon site, The Castles, The English Civil War and Mary Queen Of Scots; on the top loading bay there is yet another plaque briefly describing history of the site.

Meanwhile at the Manor Lodge (Castle), open days are held throughout the summer months, on a typical open day there are guided tours of the site, re-enactments of battles etc, falconry, people in historical costumes, sometimes a look around the Turret House etc, usually the open days are on a Sunday 11am till 4pm.

At the same time as informing the reader of the City's history, I have set out to try and get each individual to let their imagination run wild, this may lead to let's say, stand and imaging (or try) when they are down at the

Castle Market area, what the place would have looked like at the time of the Saxons, the Lovetot's Castle burnt to the ground along with the town itself, the Furnival's Castle being built, Mary Queen of Scots, cannons firing in the English Civil War, whilst walking around the market (inside and outside) wondering which part of the castle you would have been stood in. Is it or indeed was it the very spot where Mary Queen of Scots was kept prisoner? What would people from centuries ago say or think if they could come and see what we have got today? Where they knew the Castles and their dwellings once stood centuries ago in their world, long before ours.

If they did think about the future, and I suppose they did, surely not in their wildest dreams could they imagine it turning out the way it has done.

How the Royalists in the Castle at the time of the English Civil war must have been desperate for more Fire Power against the Parliamentarian Soldiers; who knows if there had been more fire power available we may still have had a castle still standing today, instead of Castle Market. When they looked up into the sky from inside the Castle no way would they have known that just a few hundred years later, you and I on the very same spot would be looking at maybe an aeroplane or a helicopter when we are out shopping.

This work has been computer generated by K. Sidebottom, all rights reserved and copyright 2005

Cover illustration by Elizabeth Mottram